My Koans
-Musings of Life-

AADYA YADAV

INDIA · SINGAPORE · MALAYSIA

ISBN 979-8-89233-514-0

ଓଃଓ

DEDICATION

This collection of poems is dedicated to *my glorious mother*, *amazing father*, and *my annoying* but *insightful brother*, all of whom I love very much.

ଓଃଓ

Contents

ꕥ

Preface

ઌ✾ઌ

A Koan is a riddle Buddhist monks use to understand and contemplate the truths of life. Koans don't have answers but prompt a person to think beyond right and wrong and their limited scope.

Life, much like koans, is grey. Right and wrong are subjective, and the only true reality is one's perspective of life. It's meant to be experienced by intuition rather than logic. My work explores feelings and sparks felt in the human experience, the truth. My truth and perhaps yours.

I hope you can find a home in my words; I hope they make you feel.

Acknowledgements

I'd like to extend my gratitude to the creator of everything. Thank you for this beautiful life, this gift of writing that I hold so dear, and the ability to perceive all the beauty you have created, along with the opportunity to do so.

I am but my parents' child, being the youngest child of my family; I happen to have three. I wouldn't be who I am if not for them, and I owe my life to them.

I would also like to thank my grandma for the magic I inherited from her poems. I owe my inspiration to the books and comics my father so fondly got for me, the worlds my brother introduced me to in games, books, TV alike, and of course, the magical tale-weaving of my mother.

Clueless

ᔓᔕ✽ᔓᔕ

All the beliefs I held
They were not right.
My world is turning upside down,
I don't know whether to laugh or frown.

I have at the least been blindsided,
There goes my claim of being far sighted.
At the most, played like a joke
'Come on, world, raise your toast'.

All I had was in my head,
Nothing there is ever right.
My right brain left and the left ain't right.
My demons and I—we're really tight.

When I am absurdly sure,
Reality kicks down all doors.
All new vision I can see,
I feel so stupid; lost at sea.

I don't know North.
East or west?
I can't recognise at sea,
But the south always beckons me.

Wherever I swim,
the tides shall turn.
So clueless
in this world under the sun.

A blind darkness
makes me come undone.
No sense does this maze make,
Might be fun for those who can play.

I don't wanna be wrong.
But I can't do what's right.
Strive to be better.
But I can't put up a fight.

All my senses are as good as none.
Someone must be having a lot of fun.
I lost the manual; the rules are unknown.

But I just might figure out how to move my pawns.

Resilience

ఆ❈ఆ

I saw a leaf
Floating in the air
Coming down to earth
At my feet
Loud footsteps,
Coming down the street
With a crunch, they recede
Beyond the scenery.
I look up at
An old, balding tree.
Its bark had grown.
As strong as a shield
It must have seen a few
Hundred summers,
Hundred rainstorms,
And some hundred thunders.
Yet look at the almighty god.
Standing so pathetically still
As all its leaves, turn in their sleep
Brown and dull with grief

You and I
Aren't all that different.
Adversity cuts us down to size.
Our edges grow dull with passing time.
And there are times when
We can't do anything about it
But if we survive for just one more season,
We'll be blooming again, dear.

Lost wonder

ᔓᔕ❃ᔓᔕ

I had plans
Drawn unclear
But I had them.
Residing besides my heart
I had dreams
Though blurry
I'd hurry
To note them as I woke
Every morning
I woke up with new hope
Went to bed
With renewed zest
Those days
Are far behind now
I find it hard
To get out of bed
I don't want to walk barefoot
In the hot or cold sand
Don't feel like having ice cream in winter.

Something has taken over me, something sinister.
When I look around,
To find out
I got 'age' as an answer
but, as I dug a little deeper
Something worse than lessened senses was playing games,
they had won because I left myself defenceless
Neglected the fort, had it fend for itself
Now it wanted revenge.
So, once a wonder,
full of wonder, now wanders
through the world's wonders
without blinking once.
As soon as the realisation hit
I tried to find a fix
For this curse, this jinx
I needed to mend it.
Because these breaths
They don't feel like mine,
They're too rhythmic,
too much in sync, in line.
I'm living a nightmare.
Once upon a time, my worst fears

have come true.
I hope some lessons from moral values would
come through.
But I see no outstretched hand,
An aid is just a dream.
I'm stuck in a labyrinth,
A prison of my mind.
I built these walls,
And christened them mine.
Now I'll slowly poke holes,
To let some air into my lungs.
To feel alive,
One more time,
Just this once.

Only Me

❦

I want someone to blame.
Make it seem like
All my problems
Are, somehow, their mistakes.
I want to point my finger
And name all my sins his.
Someone I can easily push away,
Someone who will carry my weight.
I know it's like the Curse
of the Infinity Chains.
The more weight I lose,
The more guilt I gain.
Someone whose feelings don't hurt,
Someone who can wish the pain away.
Never realised actions never done,
Too had their consequences.
I wish there was someone else I could blame.

A Park Bench

ᔓᔕ✽ᔓᔕ

It was no secret.
I sat there, breaking
Hands cold
With no one to hold.

You held your hands out.
But I couldn't see it.
I tried to shout,
But you didn't hear it.

I hugged myself.
To warm my chilled bones
And you sat there, waiting.
Right next to me.

You were hopeless,
As the load broke your spine,
You forgot to give a genuine smile.
and I was distant.

Sitting on the same bench, both suffering.
Despite knowing fully well,
We were bleeding, and our wounds never healing.
Couldn't help each other.

Sat on the shared bench.
Miserable and all alone.
couldn't find a soul.
To help us out of this hole.

Help each other?
Too scared to tend to our scars.
Each touch (try) was painful.
Was there ever anything we could do?

True Emotions

ഗ❀ഗ

I yearn for a true emotion to feel.
Something so raw,
So fun to dwell in for hours and hours.
Any emotion, just true, I need.
I yearn for a true emotion to feel.
One that is so real to me
That it seems fake.
A lie of reality.
I yearn, and I pray
But always, regardless of my will,
I feel my emotions,
Overwhelming yet tainted.
No satisfaction I find
In laughter, in cries
All seem incomplete.
Fraudulent, complete lies.
A perfect emotion
That fills me with warmth. Like a baggy
sweater,
always a little uncomfortable.

but the feeling, incomparable.
I yearn for a true emotion to feel.
To swim, to drown, to revel in all its glory
Feel high or feel low,
I yearn for a true emotion to feel.
They escape me.

Below The Barren Willow Tree

ও❦ও

Down by the mountain
Across the wood's creek
Below the barren willow tree
Lurk, the monsters of the night
Seeking blood, it seems.
A thump, a thud, and a rattling sound
Sends the heart flying
'Something in your throat' they say.
As you try to make a sound,
Legs freeze up, cramped, you feel
It's a gruesome end; you're doomed to meet.
Their shadows are creeping closer.
Your fear is what they want.
It gives them pleasure, you see.
They seem to mock your cowardice.
As they slowly stagger closer
You hear the heavy footsteps, clogging up your senses.
You can't seem to focus.

Everything's a blur.
As your life flashes by
You think to yourself
Oh, why, oh, why
Oh why?
Why didn't I listen,
Why did I come?
As your screams fill the forest
The monsters howl in relish.
Yet another troubling case to be solved,
Down by the mountain
Across the wood's creek
Below the barren willow tree.

The Clearing

‘Two miles in, on the yellow road’ they said.
‘To your right after the cotton candy hut’.
That’s the way to the fountain.
That’s overflowing with love and comfort.
But it’s been a while since I set out.
Loneliness has got me talking to the shadows now.
I’m in a forest I don’t recognise.
Can’t remember if it was left or if it was right
Now, I don’t know where I’m headed.
Not trusting my gut, I was a fool.
My path is covered in fog.
I can’t see straight.
But if I’m really being honest,
I’ve never felt better than this.
Many unsettling emotions
Are swirling in my chest.
This might be good, or this might be bad.
But my destination’s never been clearer.
I see the light ahead.
The hope, the faith—it makes me glad.

Brief of War-Fate

ഗ❦ഗ

I saw a castle.
Standing in half
The glory
It represented once
Broken mantles
Fragmented arcs
Thousands of beautiful vases
Their existence now just shards
O king!
Look at what you are now.
Oh! What all you held dear
Is no longer beautiful art.
Your bones are trophies.
That adorns someone's home.
With pride, they wear
Your defeat, like crowns.
Another kingdom fell.
Legacies lost,
Families, people whole, morals, spirits,
destroyed

Each home is a horror show.
They hold parties.
For victory, and it's victors
clink Cheers! We have killed them all!
In the shadows boils yet another meaningless war.
For me, fate, or call me destiny
Time flies quite quickly.
Just a second later, after their laughs have been bellowed
Their corpses lie battered, nameless, unknown.
Meanwhile, on the horizon
Yet another victory party is thrown.
And on and so on.
Life in mindless conflict goes on.

Self-care

ꕥ

Beauty is in the eye of the beholder.
So you better not falter.
When you compliment mine.

Cause I just might die inside.
never want to see me in your eyes.
Bit dramatic, but so what?

I already question everything I'm told.
Find good remarks to be covered flaws.
Everything is good, but there's always a but.

I changed my habits.
But my mind forgot.
Now we repeat the cycle.

Took a minute to get back my spring
A thousand sessions in my head with my
shrink,
She's decided my worth is just in being.

But, like always, there's something, and
I got over this last week, but I need
To be reminded daily.

I am fine, and life is good.
I had a lot misunderstood .
The world is what I want it to be.

A walk in the park, if fit, I see.
This life is mine, and mine alone.
I need to love myself unconditionally.

ART

ꕥ

Art, expression of life itself.
Embodiment of human strife
It's a place where emotions collide.
Presented are vague ideas,
Deciphered meaning is each to its own.
Yet the different tales all tell the same song.
In the same tone
Some of hope and some of grief
It here where all ideas thought and emotion of ours
Materialise and meet
Untangle the mess in your head.
Put it on paper instead.
Or put it on stage.
With graceful movement, tell of that
Which is felt by one and every
You and I might be different, but we all feel the same.
That is why expression of oneself – art,
Is the expression of life itself.

Lost

ജ✽ഗ

I feel lost,
I see the world around me.
drowning in colourful glory
but nothing feels like home here to me.
I see dark,
in a brightly lit room
I sit, lost in space.
Trying to find my way, trying to find my place.
I once heard, 'we are lost stars,
trying to light up the darkness.'
Never before have words been so apt.
perfectly portray what I felt.
The feeling of not being lost alone,
is little comfort to the little me in solitude.
What is a lost child to communicate to?
Even in a crowd, I'm lost all alone.
Feelings and thoughts are all incomplete.
Mind flies at lightning speed.
Doesn't want to live in a place
that doesn't feel like home.

I read that
The most trouble is a lost soul.
As I wander on a path
I wonder where it'll lead me.
Like a blind man, I test my surroundings.
not really comprehending anything.
I wander aimlessly and look through soullessly.
at the beauty, the ones before me have built.

Hoping it strikes me with purpose,
something I have never felt,
but I have this hollow.
I try to find a piece that fits.
Fit it with something fitting,
so nothing feels amiss,
but I am a lost child.
I don't know what I look for.
I see around me a lot of beauty,
passion and competence attract,
they shine brighter than Polaris.
Just the same, I can't reach them.
I'm a lost child, and the world is passing me by,
destiny has neglected my cry,
time shrugged me off and
fate has left me at a crossroad of crossroads.

I’m a lost soul,
I’ll sit here for a while.
Maybe I’ll drift with the wind
and find something worth the while.

The Real Plot

ᘓ❃ᘓ

Morals, principal
All sacrificed
In the end,
To make it right,
Lose yourself
And save them all
Is it just me?
Or does the hero always fall
The villains know not the madness
Of being wronged when being right
It's the broken heroes
That need saving, not the irrevocably cracked world.

Life

ഗ✽ഗ

I was once told that 'ships in the harbour are
safe,
but that's not what they are built for'
even a fragile butterfly can
such a rigid cocoon break
so what do we have to be afraid of
it is our battle we must fight
we have to wake the beast to know it's
intention
not just assume
and act on assumptions
for if all is not what it seems to be
life. Really, is a simple thing.

My Little Secret

ꕥ

Sometimes I'd keep quiet
Just so I could hear you smile.
I Didn't always like it
But your happiness was worth the while.

Where The Sun and The Sky Meets

ഗ✽ഗ

As long as I remember
I was staring at the sea
The line where the sky and sea used to meet.
It was a beautiful sight
that would give me relief
from the worldly thing and seniority.
It looked like an endless hope
residing inside me.
A new day, a new hope, a new desire is born everyday
at the line where the sky
and the sea used to meet each day.

Death's First Meeting

ღ✾ღ

After days and days of waiting,
I think I've had lough
After days and days of crying
I think I'm ready to forget your/you love
After weeks of staring
Into the deep blue sky
I think I've found the happiness
That I found in your smile.
After years and years of caring,
Of what happened to you
I finally realise all these feelings,
Are all in vain to you
Cause you have gone far away
And we might not meet again.
For a thousand more days.
I hope you're ok.
Cause I don't feel the same!
I wonder where you are
Probably somewhere amongst the stars

Nytx

ଓঃ❀ଓঃ

At night
look at the starry skies
can't help wondering why?
At night
Look at the glowing moon
Always changing its mood to suit the colours
Of the starry hues.
At night,
Look at it and wonder how
Something so quiet
Look so nice
Be so dark
And still light up the whole sky

Little Girl

ᔕ✽ᔕ

Little girl,
What are you afraid of
Little girl,
Why are you quivering in the shadows?
Little girl,
Do you know what your future holds?
Little girl,
What are you thinking
You can tell me, I promise I'll understand
It's not like you can lie to yourself (right?).
Little girl,
don't you smile?
Tell me why you don't smile these days.
It's been a while since I saw your face lit.
Little girl,
Tell me what I should do
Feels like I always fail when I try to improve.
I'm stuck in a hole
And I can't get out

No none seems to understand me, even when I shout
Little girl,
you're my help, my only aid.
So little girl,
Tell me why I can't smile these days,
Why is it that in these tough times
Am I stuck talking to myself
Note: little me, I wish you well.

Scared

ℰ✽ℰ

As she lay on her bed,
Asleep
The shadows on here room wall,
Creep
She blinked one of her eyes open
Just to make sure that
The man isn't back,
To watch her sleep.
What she saw,
Horrified her
The man was there with his crooked smile
The one that made sure
She was terrified
Her father had assured her
That the man who terrified her
Had died
And that's when she decided
it was better not to hide.
She screamed with terror
When she grabbed her ankle

No, she was sure that her father had
Not make an error,
She could feel his hand
Cold and smoky
Very much dead.
Just like her, now.

Sirens

ೞ✽ೞ

Hey little child, little child
Won't you follow me
Hey little child, little child
Wake from your sweet dreams.
Hear my voice, seek it
What sweet melody.
March at the chant
to the deep blue foamy sea.
The moon is high
Tides clashing
Magic's in the air.
Don't stop walking
Till you hear the voices closing in
Don't worry, don't shut your ears
We won't hurt you dear.
Don't fear me
They are just stories
of people lost at sea.
It's true I'm the beauty
From those fantasies

But what you know about me
Are just tales, someone's wild dream.
Reach forward
Don't you wanna see.
my enticing world
Under the sea
So take my hand
we'll go together, will fall free
(that's more like it)
Now count to three.
Till your soul's mine for keeping
for the rest of eternity.

A Magical Place

ঌ✽ঌ

The harbour is never quiet
It's so full of life
So many people with their jolly faces
Some with dejected sighs painted
One too many drunk people by the seaside
Washing their sorrows away with the tides
Confiding in the screaming silence
of the night sky.
There are families waiving their goodbyes
Some with big ol' smiles,
While others cry
Bidding adieu to their loved ones
Knowing they'll not meet for a while
Behind it's plain disguise
So many stories and secrets it hides
The place itself is alive
Breathing and feeding on memories left behind.

Stump

ఌ✽ఌ

I'm not sure where I'm headed
Unsure what I want
I know it may sound like an excuse
But I got the wall in front of me
Impenetrable, it seems(to me)
I've got all the tool and all the things
I could ever need but to scale this monstrosity
I don't have the will
The will to do anything.

Healing

ᘓᘐ✾ᘓᘐ

Before I go through with it,
While I'm doing it
Not always after.
I know I'm wrong
but I do it anyway.
It's killing me,
I'm incompetent,
Act it out with nonchalance
Covering it up with defiance.
Wrong, false, fraudulent facade.
No longer I can't take it,
My own darkness
Is suffocating.
I need to leave
This dark playground
That I built for my guilt,
I see the light to guide me
I need to follow it.
No more hold ups
I'm ready for greatness

I'll take flight
And own the sky.

My Truth

ശ❀ശ

In the meadows
Far away from what our eyes can see.
You tell me it's a world fantasy,
"It's imaginary."
What you don't get,
Is that it is all that there is.
To me.

Blind

෴❀෴

It hurt so bad
I thought you knew
I was wishing that
You'd know what words to use
But I understand
Life doesn't go the way
We plan it to

But still I'd hoped
That things would change
Why would I count on you
When habits rarely break
But even now and even then

When it happens again
I'd still be looking at you
To help me through
And understand.

Feed Up-Disturbed

ഗ❀ഗ

Anytime now
I'm gonna snap
The older I get
The more I get sad

Never really felt it
So deep in my bones
Now it feels like
It's never going to let me go

It's getting hard to breath
My brain can make no sense
So all it does is repeat
Self pity, self hate nonsense

I'm always on the edge
I'm hard to deal with
I come off snobbish
But really I'm just hurt.

Human Life

(Haiku)

ଓଃ❃ଓଃ

Mortality, Life is a struggle
And in the end we can die
Go ahead, ignore this poem.

History of Our Cities

Burning, heroes are falling
Raining on our cities
With their last stands

The stories, never told
And never saw the light
Were deemed to be horrors
Monsters, unspoken of

Roaming the streets
Eyes speaks
More than the deafening silence
Blind ear we turn to the screams

Pretend, a world of fraudulence
Live blissfully
In castles of bones
And tears hardened to stones

On the burning horizon
For how long can skeletons be hidden
Soon the truth will be seen
Searing on the scene

Flashing, like a big mistake
Do a double take
Take them to your grave
Our cities are built on smiles fake.

Death

ᔓᔕ✽ᔓᔕ

Death I've know is universal
But at my age it's almost impossible
I could be 8 or 18 or 80
Even at my last breath I wouldn't believe

As my source withers and trembles
I'll still hold on with all the might
All that I could muster
What a wicked game, I'm bound to lose

Proposal is immodest
Painted in Unfair terms
Yet I an addict
Can't get enough

Nothing I'll take to my grave
Yet all these desires I crave
Closer to death every second
But planning on next night next day

I'll be gone
And knowing will mean nothing
Not just me but trillions before
Have died and lived with no fruitful bounty

Called it a chore
Nothing to be done
Just something to ponder
What a drug, trying to live is killing us.

My Necessity

ᔓᔕ✽ᔓᔕ

I can't believe that this is all that there is in this world
There has to be an alternate reality
Existing breathing thriving just an inch out of reach
This is a fantasy in which I do, I really do need to believe.

Where Am I?

Where am I?
Not here for sure

I'm there
But never quite there anymore

I'm on a beach
A quite seashore

The violent tides are crashing
Glimpsing into my state of being

Of never being
just at one place anymore

I'm here
But where could that be?

Being right now,
My existence fights with the duelling realities

In my mind I'm here no-more
But god knows I can never fully let go

There and Back
And here again

Always there just never quite here
Where am I? I wonder

Where could I be? I struggle.
Again and again.

Maybe I Should Go?

꧁❀꧂

I love you But
I don't love myself
When I'm around you

Cause no matter what I say
You hold a steady haze
As though you're staring into silence

Only so long
can I not mind it
I might've fooled you but I'm not blinded

Tried many different cures
I can no longer deny
I'm trying to hide and

You will never know
How you hurt Me
Why I bleed so

You will be indifferent
To all my screams
And I'll still keep screaming

Waiting on a single flinch
Never losing hope
I want to give up believing

How much longer can I hold
I'm hanging by a thread
Unable, but begging myself to let go.

My Love Story

When love wasn't around the corner
I knew love wasn't for me
Cause when I looked all over for her
She was nowhere to be seen

But even now when I close my eyes
The fantasies they take me
To a world build better
Built for a love for me

And the stories they keep me up at night
The tales of all that could be
But when I walk these streets
Back home I am greeted with reality

A love like the movies
One where'd they'd cross the seas
Love like the books
Living after death immortally

A love that I have know
Is not the love I seek
A custom tailor made fit
Just like my wild dreams

The love I look for
The love I seek
Is a love I'll never have
Cause in a perfectly imperfect love I believe

Whiplash life

ᔕ❀ᔕ

Some days I feel so high
Could jump over the moon
Other days the tides hold me closer
Washing me deeper than before

Weight of the ocean on me
Wings to be amongst the clouds
Feel the sun on my face
But the darkness stings my back

Deep breaths and I feel grounded
Single word triggers
Turn carpet to quick sand
Falling through faster than I can count

1,2 down the rabbit hole
3 million times already
Can't get enough of both realities
Keep coming back to each

To My Bestie

ᔓᔕ✾ᔓᔕ

Year after year
I hope that you're there
Right here next to me

Through the troubled water
Through dark times
Into the light
Saying we'll be fine

Oh friend
I hope
Till the end of time
I'm still yours to call mine

Simpler Life

ಌ✽ಌ

Can't it just be feel good
Why is it gotta mean so much
Can we just be the sweet-sweet
From the heartfelt movies that we love

Can this just be easy
Like slipping on ice
Can our adventures be smooth
Like skating on cream on a rainbow cloud

I know it is rough
To be, just be you
When if feel as if all is on the line
Can we just be carefree
Not care about a thing

Like those lovely slice of life Webtoons.

Frustration

(Haikyuu)

ᏧᏍ✾ᏧᏍ

I scream into the darkness,
As one would expect and one knows
There indeed is no reply.

An Old Friend

ᘓᘐ✽ᘓᘐ

A piece of my past is coming to me,
We shall meet and greet.
Damp air, thundering clouds
Loom like shadows of past deeds, memories.

Maybe a sunny day
With dancing daisies
And prancing puppies
with lilac hues over the horizon as far as one
can see

Whatever it maybe
It fills me the anticipation of synergy, with
So much of unnamed energy

Maybe uncertainty,
With clouds of doubt
Along with insuppressible Glee.

Am I Wrong?

ᔓᔕ❃ᔓᔕ

Sometimes I feel so insignificant
Like what I say don't even matter
I don't know if I should just quit
Or pretend I don't care

If you were someone else
I might not care a bit,
But you being you
Has got something over me

I care too much, ain't that rich.
I am always so conflicted
Can't make my own decision
Indecisive I can't help it

It's my nature
you say I exaggerate
But I'm just stuck in my mind
In my thoughts I rewind
Everything, Every time

If something could have changed the outcome
Would I change it
I'm so confused
Ain't sure what to do

What to feel and what not to
Tell me where I'm wrong
If you can truly mean it
Am I wrong?

Living in Pictures

ಽ❃ಽ

I'm scared of leaving,
Just a bit.
I tend to forget everything.
So I wonder,
Will this place be a fantasy?
For me, like the last one is now.
They all seem like a dream
Like I'm missing something,
Maybe a touch of reality
But I know what I've seen and felt.
It was real
Just feels surreal in my messed up head.
I'm scared of leaving
What if I forget?
The time, the laughs
The everything?
That mattered so much then.
What if it becomes a lore forgotten by time?
I wanna remember
So I tend to live in picture and in the past,

It's my way of memorising memories
So I know they'll last
But the fear doesn't end
And the satisfaction doesn't last.

Growing Up

ೞ✽ೞ

This is it, I'm growing up
I did the justifiable thing
But it's not enough

I must do so much more
But there exist no such door
Where the fairy tale end can come through

So rough edged existence
Thumbed at the edges silence
With age we learn a new way

Learn that there are no perfect solutions
No matter how much you wish
It is what it is.

My decision leaves me unsettled
Leaves my love unfinished
But I must do the rational thing cause nothing else fits

Can't we go back to a time
When We weren't so serious
I guess it's too late.

You wouldn't hear me
Think me blind not to see
But I stood where you stand

I've grown, yes
But life's teaching me anew
How to be the bigger man

How to be silent when your mind screams
Accept things all against your believes
Learn to let go,
Each time, a piece of your soul.

Now I do it before I can be forced
Yes I have grown
It might seem sad now
But when you know, you'll know.

Where Am I? Part II

ంঃఁ

Glass eyed I sit
Always right here
Where else could I go?

You see me but you don't
See me seeing through it all.
Do you?

You can tell I'm not here,
Every time that I'm there.
But you got used to letting that go

You can never feel,
Never truly see the world
That I lose sight of.

To you this is it,
All that there is
And I'm being disrespectful

But this can't be all
Not for me I need more
I demand something, I can't recall anymore.

And then you look at me
And I feel the need to feel
Once more

Quite steadily, I barely let go
Forgetting I can never exist here
Not fully anymore

pieces of me float in another plane.
I'll be back here again.
I can never let go or 'Wouldn't' as I'm told.

Kids Do Know Better

ઊ❃ઊ

I remember a time
When you were mine
And there is nothing sweeter, better
Than our memories
Together.

We promised forever
Knowing it don't last long,
We sang our last song.

I Wonder

ᔕᔓ✽ᔕᔓ

Sometimes I wonder
If you hear the words you say,
I wonder if you ever really cared
Or is it all in my head

A desperate fantasy,
Equivalent to a meaningless unrealistic dream
You seem there, but are you listening
Or am I just crazy, over dramatic?

Screaming at a screen
Cause my words don't seem to be reaching
You
I don't know if you care

And it's driving me mad
Should I believe your actions
Or what everyone else says?

A Blue Day

ఌ✽ఌ

I feel lost
I know I'm wrong
But I can't quit
Like that 'stuck In The head for the whole day'
song
I don't know where I should go
Can't seem to tell myself no

I can't even finish this song

Perspective

ᔓᔕ❃ᔓᔕ

I've walked the roads
I've been here before
I have seen
All the ways, that you talk of

But i did not see
All that you saw
my feet too have marked these alleys
As their own

Nevertheless, we walk not the same road
We share the places and names
But our stories speak in stark contrast

I have seen
And you have too
But our minds saw what our eyes could not
Only on this we can agree

A Story In The Mountains

ᔕ❀ᔕ

Gliding on the road
I saw the river snaking adjacent
How glorious it looked
Set deep in pits green
Surrounded by emerald giants
Guarding its treasure
It glimmers in the hot sun
Lighting up the sky
Crystal blue spotted with wisps magical
The giants jutted tiny houses
In pastel and in bold
So many stories in the hills
All mystical fantasies to behold.

Talking With The Giants

ଓ✽ଓ

The giants are staring down at us
Beware! Beware!
Their wrath but know well their love

The mountains are calling
Beaconing our souls
Be steady but be fast
Be ready to lose your soul

Recognise yourself as an artist if you may
But know your not a thing
Without their embrace
Can you hold their cold gaze?

They will say not a word
But poetry will be woven
In the morning song
In the fog, in the trees

Very clearly you will see
A language you never knew–So fluent, so sweet
Straight to your core it will sting and soothe
The same you too would like to speak.

I Wanna Draw Houses

ℰ✽ℰ

I wanna draw houses
Houses with the stories
Shimmering with the glory
Left from golden days

I wanna write a poem
About all that was
Who lived, who died, who loved
No matter what the genre is

I'm talking about the houses
Houses that are, were, will be homes one day
With the splash of character
Memories that speak through the walls

Give me balconies looking over hills
A drab half standing one, on a barren hill
The beach side, sunny pastel
Or a one that looks like it houses a hidden
crypt

I wanna draw houses
Tell all of their stories
Can no longer keep it inside me
The voices they're shouting

Wishing to be heard
Willing to be seen
Under a painter's brush
They will finally rest, paused in a moment of time, recounting their story.

Mother River

ᔕ❃ᔕ

Mother river
I look your way
I await your grace
The first step and each that follows
I'll wait another year
Just to see you again
From afar, as close as I can be
I know you'll return
You too wait patiently
To meet me
It's been long enough soon we will reconcile
My poetry and your lapping waves
Azure you have painted me
Without you, blue I feel.
Can I ever be complete
Without you blessing me
Mother river I sit at your banks
Seeking answers from your realm
Tell me of the calm and tranquillity
Of what you are made.

Tell me what made you so fierce
So I too can be same
Soft to those that are mine
And unforgiving in my art
Your grace and beauty
Grant me
A part of all that your are
So I can be all that I ever can be.

Trees On A Hill

ঔৣ❀ঔৣ

And what are you doing there
Standing so still
Looking at us all passing by
You've lived not so long
You look so wise
Tell me too
The tales you have seen
Tell me what goes on the hill
Between you and your friends
Who is stronger
Who has lived longer
Whom have you lost
How are you still holding on
So young so ripe
Give me too an ounce of your might.

Foggy Mountain

Shrouded you stand
Tall
Foreign to me
I know already know all that there is to see
But every time I'm still struck by your beauty
You remind me how tiny I am
So perfectly still but your body speaks volumes
About all that there is
An existential feeling left in my heart
Left yearning for something unknown unseen
You are mystic, the magic
That drives the very soul to fight to be seen
So imposing so intimidating
But so lovely
How grand of a deity
Perfect in every sense
You never apologise for the space you take
never bow to nobody
You know your place
Your happy with you grace

No matter how you are seen or
Your value deemed
Your confidence strikes a feeling deep
Deep I feel it in my bones
My core need to let some things go
A part of me wants to be able to breathe
As you so
So uniquely you
A gorgeous stance to take.
A thing to lose for, to put all at stake
What a good hill to die on.

Us

ઈ✾ઈ

We've got such a long way to go
So many roads yet to take
I can't tell you where this'll lead

Me to you, you to another state
State of mind or a physical line that none can break
This journey is long and we'll never know
Where it'll take Each and every

Each turn is a make or break
Kind of scene
We may meet again
Or be never again to be seen

The ways will wind up and down
Might even turn around
But will I be at the same crossroads
Even then

Will I be lost
Will I see where this goes
Will I be calm
Will we all lose control

It'll be a wild ride, that much is for sure
Not always smooth I'm told
But in this moment I know you
And for us I'll hold out hope.

Destruction Through Time

ꕥ

They laid waste to the land
Waste to the land
Ohh, ohh.
They came they plundered,
They conquered.
Oh oh, oh oh.
They laid waste to the land,
Waste to the land
Of the people.
No love, no glory lived.
They lay waste to the land,
Waste to my land.
These skyscrapers built on graves.

Back Again

ඏ✽ඏ

Word, word, word
Oh my word
I can't tell you how this feels

I'm in a world
I forgot I'd ever need
It feels like someone's speaking to my soul

Like I've come back home,
And all these corners I know so well
A shadow of how I was and now who I've
become

I see it in the mirrors
All that I'd ever been
I see myself clearer
Now that I see again the child in me

This place I swore never to forget
By accident I stand where I stood

I am no more of a man
Than I'd been when I was ten
Thank you for taking me home

I fit finally
Right where I belong
Sitting on the stairs writing my little poems
Writing of worlds you'd never know.

It's Not Personal, No.

❦

It's not personal, no
Don't make it so
Take it as if watching in through window
Your favourite comedy show
The disasters are just plot twists
Your mistakes - comedic relief
Life is so much easier as a comedy piece.

Let Them Be

ᏋᏍ✽ᏋᏍ

Let the songs sing their song
Let them preach what they preach
We'll dance to our own melody
They've been here longer and they know
But I say, I know you
And I know me
Lets make our own symphony
Escape this orchestrated orchestra
And find a place for you and me
Won't you keep me company
In a world of new music
We could be all that there is
Swaying with the wind
Let's be legendary.

Welcome to My Art

❦

I don't wanna be lost in the crowd
I wanna be lost in the clouds
I wanna be lost in another world
Not have me lost on this world

I wanna be lost in the scene
but you won't be able to ignore me
Cause my voice, it will roar
Like a lion in the Artic

Wildfire in Antarctica
You'll see
Whether you will it
Or not, ain't a choice

Blinded by the sight
I'll have the world kneel
To my visions, to my dreams
Indulge in my reality

Unique, make people sceptic
Put things in Different perspective
Just see the world in fragments
Stained glass of mediaeval churches

all that could be
Should be, would be
Tales of magic
In this world but out of this reality

I plan to captivate through
My art shrouded in mystery
Welcome to A new world
to be discovered, to be truly seen.

Author's Note

ꕥ

Thank you.

Hope you enjoyed your stay and that we'll see you again soon.

With love and best wishes.

www.ingramcontent.com/pod-product-compliance
Lightning Source LLC
La Vergne TN
LVHW091116150826
845673LV00002B/855

* 9 7 9 8 8 9 2 3 3 5 1 4 0 *